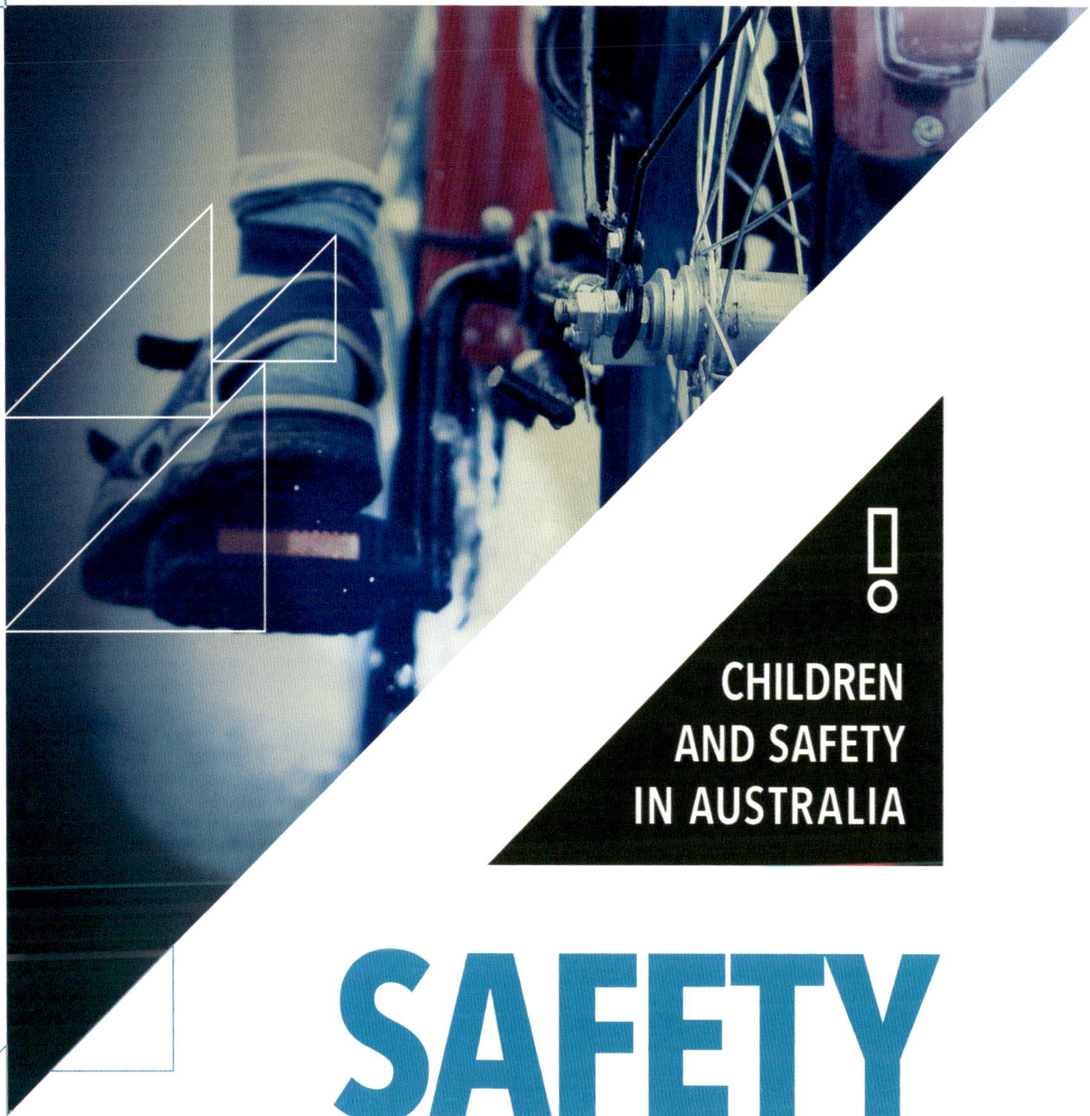

CHILDREN AND SAFETY IN AUSTRALIA

SAFETY AWAY FROM HOME

WILLIAM DAY

Redback Publishing
PO Box 357 Frenchs Forest NSW 2086
Australia

www.redbackpublishing.com.au
orders@redbackpublishing.com.au

978-1-925630-66-4

Author: William Day
Editor: Marianne Lindsell
Designer: Redback Publishing

Original illustrations © Redback Publishing 2018
Originated by Redback Publishing

Printed and bound in China by Leo Paper

Acknowledgements
Abbreviations: l—left, r—right, b—bottom, t—top, c—centre, m—middle
We would like to thank the following for permission to reproduce photographs:
(Images © shutterstock)

Every effort has been made to contact copyright holders of any material reproduced in this book. Any omissions will be rectified in subsequent printings if notice is given to the publisher.

A catalogue record for this book is available from the National Library of Australia

CONTENTS

INTRODUCTION

Children who ride their bikes to school, walk to the shops by themselves, or take the bus to visit a friend's home need to be aware of a few basic safety rules. Taking care of your own safety is a part of growing up.

When you are with your family on a camping trip, the rules about keeping safe are very different from when you are at home. If a friend's family invites you to join them on a holiday, their family rules about safe behaviour could be different from ones you are used to at home. Sleepovers at a friend's home or with your aunts, uncles or grandparents can all involve learning about keeping safe in unusual situations.

Keeping safe involves using common sense and being aware of what is happening around you. If you ever feel that you or younger members of your family are in an unsafe situation, tell your parent or a trusted adult immediately.

Once you feel confident about how to stay safe, you can relax and enjoy being out and about.

WATER SAFETY

Whenever you go for a swim, never swim alone

Beaches

Australia's climate and beautiful beaches make swimming one of the most popular pastimes for children and their families.

Always choose to swim between the flags and at a beach where there are lifeguards on duty. The red and yellow flags are a signal that the lifeguards have checked the water and selected an area that is safest for swimmers to use. This means there is less risk of there being rips or undercurrents in the water that can pull a swimmer away from the shore. Lifeguards also check for holes in the sand under the waves that can suddenly trap an unwary swimmer in deep water.

Rivers and Lakes

Swimming in rivers and lakes is different from swimming in the ocean. People float differently in salt water, so swimmers need to be aware that they may not be as buoyant in a lake. Rivers can have fast-flowing currents that will quickly take you away from the shore.

Public Swimming Pools

- ✗ Don't run along wet tiles around the pool.
- ✗ Don't jump on top of other people in the water.
- ✗ Don't dive from a board if it is too high for you and you don't know how to land in the water correctly.

What else is in the water?

- ! In seawater swimming pools near the ocean, check that dangerous marine creatures have not been washed into the water by large waves.
- ! Sharks often swim near beaches and in rivers. Listen for announcements from lifeguards about sharks, or look out for signs saying sharks may be in the water.
- ! Bluebottle stings are very painful. Keep out of the water if you see a lot of bluebottles on the sand.
- ! Pollution, rubbish and sewage washed into the ocean, rivers and lakes after a storm can make the water dirty. Don't go swimming if you think the water is not clean.

What to do if you can't swim:

Ask your parents if you can take lessons at a swimming pool.

Ask a trusted person to teach you the difference between swimming in waves and in calm water.

Don't go into deep or fast-flowing water.

Q. I was at the beach with my friends and they wanted to go and swim where it was less crowded, outside the flagged area. They laughed at me for saying that was not safe. Who was right?

A. People who get into trouble in the water when they swim outside the flagged area place lifeguards who rescue them in danger. You were right to say what your friends did was wrong.

RIDING YOUR BIKE

There are rules for bicycle riders, and they are different for children and adults. The rules are not the same in every state of Australia, so make sure you check what they are before riding outside your own front gate. For example, some states allow bike riders to ride on pedestrian crossings, while others insist that they have to dismount and walk across with their bike.

Did You Know?
In some other countries, people riding bicycles or cars on roads keep to the right and not the left of a road or path.

Most states allow children up to 12 years old to ride their bike on a public footpath. Adults with them are not always allowed to ride on the footpath and sometimes have to ride on the road.

Approved safety helmets are a good idea, but are not compulsory in all states when riding on a footpath. Use a bike path if there is one and be courteous to people who are walking or jogging in the same area.

In country areas, children on bikes may need to share a road with cars and trucks. This places a young bike rider in a position of great responsibility. Make sure you know the road rules that apply to bike riders in your state before venturing out onto a road.

Watch out for these dangers when riding your bicycle on a footpath:

Magpies swooping down on bike riders because they see them as a threat to their chicks.

Cars coming into or out of driveways.

Stop theft by attaching your bicycle to a post or tree with a chain and lock.

Little children or pets suddenly running in front of you.

If you see another bike rider coming towards you on the footpath, use the normal road rule in Australia, which is to keep to the left side of the road or path.

A person who is deaf or blind may not be aware that you are riding a bike behind them, and they can be very startled when you suddenly ride past on the footpath. Be polite and slow down in these cases.

STRANGER DANGER

When you are allowed to go out by yourself, to visit friends or go to the movies or shops, you feel that you are finally growing up. Along with the freedom comes the responsibility to be sensible and to keep yourself safe.

Stranger Danger is a term that describes the sorts of scary and unpleasant situations that children sometimes experience when they are out by themselves or with their young friends.

Be aware and take care if a stranger does any of these things:

- **Sits too close to you when there are plenty of other free seats.**
- **Follows you.**
- **Offers you food, sweets or anything else.**
- **Stops a car near you.**
- **Touches you.**
- **Tells you they know your parents or teachers.**
- **Asks you to tell them your name or address.**

If any of these things occurs, move away quickly. Shout for help if you need to. Then tell your parent, teacher, trusted adult or a police officer what has happened.

Remember that Stranger Danger can involve people who are men, women or older children.

10
9
7
6
4
2
3
1

PLAYGROUNDS AND PARKS

Playgrounds, parks and skateboard parks are wonderful places to enjoy playing with your friends. Children who live in apartments, and don't have their own gardens to play in, need to get out to public spaces where they can do lots of exercise to keep them happy and healthy.

Using a Playground

- ✓ Share the playground equipment.
- ✓ Wear a helmet as well as knee and elbow pads when using roller skates or a skateboard.
- ✓ Merry-go-rounds and see-saws are great fun. Be sensible playing on them. If another child is on the end of the see-saw, don't jump off quickly, as they might fall and hurt themselves because of what you did.

Here are some tips to keep you safe while you are enjoying the open space:

ROAD SAFETY

Pedestrian crossings

Knowing how to cross a road safely is a skill children learn as a part of growing up. Near schools during school hours, the school crossing supervisor holds up a sign to tell all the drivers to stop so that people can cross the road. If you are trying to cross a road that is not near your school, and there is no crossing supervisor to stop the cars, you need to follow some simple rules to ensure you stay safe.

If there are traffic lights, wait until the green light appears that tells you it is safe to cross the road. At a pedestrian crossing where there are no traffic lights, cars are supposed to stop to let you cross. Drivers don't always stop and sometimes they may not even see you. Always wait before you cross and make sure that the cars have stopped before you step onto the road to get to the other side. Walk quickly but don't run, in case you trip and fall.

If there is more than one lane of cars at the crossing, check as you walk across that each lane of cars is stopping. Sometimes a driver might not see you crossing if you are hidden in front of a big car or truck beside them.

If you need to cross a road where there is no marked crossing painted on the ground, stop at the kerb and look both ways before stepping onto the road.

LOOK LEFT, THEN RIGHT, THEN LEFT AGAIN

Never stop in the middle of the road. Cars move very quickly, and they will not expect you to be there. Use sight and sound to cross roads safely. You might hear a car coming around a corner before you see it. This is one reason why it is not a good idea to be listening to music with earphones when you are trying to cross a road.

Taking your dog for a walk is a job that means you have to use extra care near roads. A dog may want to run across the road to chase something, or it may want to run ahead of you. Hold on tightly to the lead and control your dog so it does not pull you onto the road. Keep the dog very close to your legs as you walk across the road to stop it wandering off sideways in front of cars.

Railway crossings

In city areas, the places where a railway line crosses a road are clearly marked and there are gates that stop anyone crossing when a train is coming. In country areas, there may not always be gates, so it is up to drivers and walkers to check very carefully when they have to cross any railway tracks. Remember that trains might be coming from both directions. A train can take about half a kilometre to stop after the driver applies the brakes.

CAMPING

Your first camping holiday in the bush is a big adventure. You may get to sleep in a tent and cook over a camp fire, or you may live in a caravan while you are on holidays.

The adults who have taken you camping will have a lot to organise, so they will be depending on you to act sensibly in the unfamiliar surroundings.

Here are some things you can do to make your camping trip the best holiday ever:

Stay near the camp. Children who disappear into the bush by themselves cause everyone else to worry about them.

There will be wild animals in the bush. Don't poke sticks into tree hollows or holes in the ground. There could be a black snake hiding inside!

To avoid getting tummy upsets, wash your hands before eating, just as you would at home.

Go swimming with another person, and only if the adults you are with have said it's OK.

Help with the cooking and washing up so everyone on the camping holiday enjoys a relaxing time.

If you are staying at a caravan park where there are public toilets and showers, be aware of Stranger Danger rules.

Sitting around a camp fire at night is one of the best things about a camping holiday. You may have never been near such a large fire before, so be aware of its dangers.

Pots that have been sitting on the camp fire, or even just hot ashes, will be very hot and will burn your hand if you pick them up.

Loose clothes near an open fire can easily catch alight.

When you are inside your tent, close the zipper to keep out little wild creatures that may try to crawl in and join you.

Help to make sure the camp fire is completely out before you leave the camp site.

WILD AND DOMESTIC ANIMALS

There are many animals to avoid in Australia, both on land and in the water.

Crocodiles

Crocodiles are a protected species across the northern waterways of Australia. They can be in the surf at beaches, and in billabongs, rivers and lakes. Crocodiles hide under the water waiting for their prey to come near the edge. If a person strays into its territory, a crocodile will attack them.

Feral dogs

Feral dogs kill livestock and native animals. Sometimes they have little fear of humans. They hunt in packs and can pose a threat to children.

Spiders

Spiders have an important role in the natural ecosystem. There are many poisonous spiders in Australia. Trap-door spiders build little burrows in the ground with a tiny door at the top. Their venom is dangerous to humans. Funnel-web spiders and redbacks are two more sorts of spiders that people should avoid.

Snakes

Australia offers perfect habitats for many species of poisonous snakes. When walking in the bush or outback, always wear strong footwear and long socks to cover the legs. Anyone who pokes a stick into a hole or hollow log is asking for trouble.

Wild Pigs

An adult wild pig is one of the most dangerous animals in Australia. It will attack a human with its tusks.

Dingoes

In most areas, wild dingoes are shy and will avoid humans. However, in areas where there are many tourists, and the dingoes have learned that some of them offer food, dingoes are more bold. These areas include Uluru in central Australia, and Fraser Island. The dingoes on Fraser Island can be such a nuisance to tourists that the authorities have issued safety guidelines for people visiting the island. Dingoes are a particular danger to small children.

Bats

Some bats in Australia carry a virus that is similar to the rabies virus. People can catch the virus by coming into contact with the bat or its droppings.

Kangaroos

Kangaroos are afraid of humans and will not usually come near them. If a large kangaroo is captured and cannot escape, it will fight and kick with its strong back legs.

Bulls

A domestic bull is a large, unpredictable animal. If you enter its paddock a bull may charge at you.

Marine Animals to Avoid

Sharks, sea-snakes, bluebottles, jellyfish, blue-ringed octopus, cone snails.

FOOD AWAY FROM HOME

At home, it is easier to make sure food is kept safe so that it does not make people sick when they eat it. This includes keeping meat cold, stopping flies sitting on food and throwing away any food that has started to rot. When you are away from home, it is not always easy to tell if food you are buying is fresh or not.

Here are some things to look for when buying food to eat while you are out and about:

- ✓ Meat must be kept cool. If the meat is sitting in the sun or in a warm room or container for a long time, it may have bacteria growing in it that will make you feel sick.
- ✓ Milk, cream and cheese can make you sick if they have been left in a warm area for too long. This is because bacteria grow in them and produce poisons.
- ✓ Check that the shop or stall where you are buying food looks clean.
- ✓ Uncooked meat should not be touching cooked meat or any other foods. If it is, go elsewhere to buy your food.
- ✓ If there are any flies on or near the food, avoid buying it.
- ✓ If any part of the food looks an unusual colour or smells strange, it may be old or have bacteria or mould growing on it.
- ✓ Sometimes shops reduce the price of older food to sell it quickly. Check that the food is still suitable to eat before you buy it.
- ✓ Fruit is a perfect choice for a snack while you are away from home. Fruit and vegetables should be washed before you eat them, as there could be bacteria on the skins.
- ✓ Clean your hands before eating, just as you should at home.

Allergies

Children with severe allergies should always have their Epipen with them.

If you are not sure what is in a meal from a shop, don't eat it.

If you are with people who don't know what your allergies are, tell them so they don't offer you the wrong sort of food.

Take extra care yourself rather than relying on other people remembering the things you are allergic to.

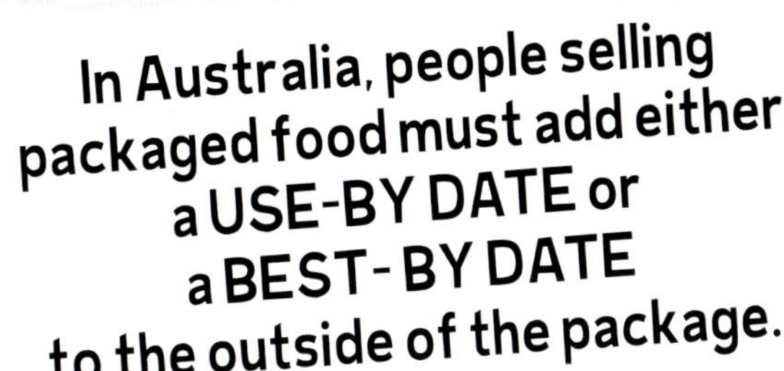

In Australia, people selling packaged food must add either a USE-BY DATE or a BEST-BY DATE to the outside of the package.

USE-BY DATES
After this date, food should not be sold and may be dangerous to eat.

BEST-BY DATES
After this date, food can still be sold as long as it is fit to eat, but it may not be of very good quality.

FLIES

Q. Flies are so tiny, they don't eat much. Why are they a problem near food?

A. Flies lay their eggs in faeces and rotting meat. They then fly to your fresh food and deposit bacteria onto it. The bacteria can make you very sick.

TRANSPORT SAFETY FOR CHILDREN

Cars

In Australia, wearing seat-belts in cars is compulsory. There are different sorts of restraints for babies, young children and adults. Car booster seats raise a child higher so that the seat-belt sits across their chest, instead of across their neck.

Children who are small should continue to use a booster seat until they are big enough so that the car's seat-belt is not across their neck.

Little children sometimes complain about being in a special child's car seat. If you have a younger brother or sister who does this, help them stay safe by making a game out of doing up the harness, or by distracting their attention with a toy.

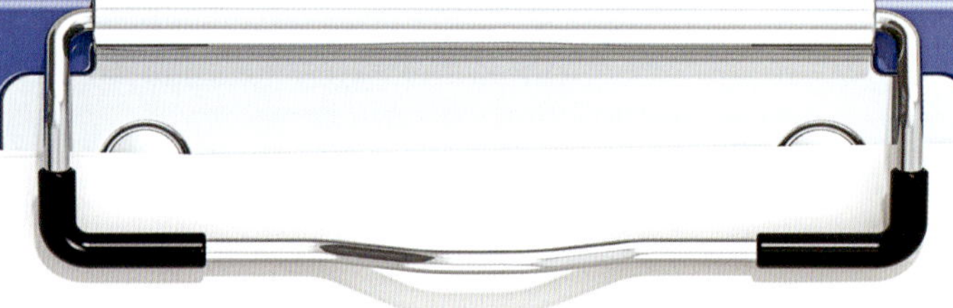

Trains

- The first time you are allowed to catch a train by yourself is an important occasion. There are lots of safety rules about riding on trains, and they apply to both children and adults.
- Stay back from the edge of the platform. Many platforms have a yellow line painted on them. No-one should cross this line until the train has stopped and you are about to enter it.
- A station platform is not a place to play games or to run. Trains are big and heavy. They cannot stop quickly if you slip over the edge of the platform. They can also hit any part of you or your belongings that are over the edge of the platform.
- When the doors open, let passengers get off the train before you try to get on it.
- The gap between the platform and the train can sometimes be wide. Be careful not to push and shove near the gap.
- Doors usually close automatically on trains. If they are faulty and stay open, keep away from the opening and hold on if you have to stand.
- Be aware of the Stranger Danger rules while you are travelling on trains.

If other people are causing trouble on the bus, move away from them if you can.

Be aware of the Stranger Danger rules while you are travelling on buses.

Sit down if there is a seat free. Hold on to a post or passenger handle if you have to stand.

Very few buses have seat belts fitted, but use them if they are available.

3uses

Vhen leaving a bus, don't try to cross the oad in front of or behind it until the bus ıas moved away. Other drivers on the road vill not be able to see that you are about o cross the road.

Leaving your bags in the aisle may result in other people falling over them and hurting themselves.

SPORT SAFETY

Team sports

Children who play team sports usually know about the correct gear to wear to keep them safe from sporting injuries. Mouthguards, pads and helmets are all important and can stop an injury occurring that would keep you away from your favourite game for weeks or longer.

Young people who play individual sports, such as athletics, depend on their coaches to recommend the correct safety gear to use.

Children who enjoy sports without a team or coach to recommend safety measures need to make sure they know about the safety rules and equipment that apply.

Fishing

Learn the correct way to cast a line into the water. The hooks are very sharp and should not be used where they can injure any person or pet either in the water or on the land nearby.

Find out the correct first-aid treatment to use if a hook gets stuck in your skin.

Take care with the sharp knives used to clean the fish you catch.

You should be able to swim if you are going to fish near the edge of a deep water jetty.

Sharks can still bite even after they are caught on a fishing line.

Rock fishing can be a dangerous sport, and anyone doing it should wear a life jacket. Many rock fishers in Australia have been washed into the sea by an unexpected large wave.

Drones

- The flying of drones is controlled by the Civil Aviation Authority in Australia.
- The height limit for the flight is 120 metres.
- You can only fly a drone during the daytime.
- You must be able to see the drone at all times.
- Keep the drone at least 30 metres away from other people.
- Drones must not be flown over beaches, sporting ovals or any place where there are a lot of people.
- You cannot fly a drone over a road accident, bushfire or other emergency situation.

SUN SAFETY

Australians love their outdoor lifestyle. One of the results of this is that we have one of the highest rates of skin cancer in the world. Everyone needs to be aware of sun safety. Getting sunburnt is painful and unsightly and has consequences that can extend throughout life. After the sunburn heals and we have forgotten about it, the damage done to our cells is hidden from us. As we get older, the rate of skin cancer increases if a person has suffered a lot of sunburn during their youth.

There are things we can do to keep our skin safe:

If you have skin that sunburns easily, wear a top over your swimsuit to protect your skin, or choose swimwear that covers your arms, neck and back.

People of all skin colours can suffer from skin cancers caused by too much sun exposure.

Wear a hat outdoors.

Wear heavy zinc cream on the main sunburn zones, like lips, nose, neck and ears.

Wear sunscreen with a high SPF rating.

Avoid being outside in the sun during the middle of the day, when the sun will burn the most.

Other Dangers From the Sun

The sun can damage our eyes as well as our kin. We all should know that it is dangerous o look directly at the sun, particularly during solar eclipse. This is because the sun is so trong that it will burn parts of the insides of our eyes.

Just being out in the sun can damage our eyes, even if we don't look directly at it. Little bumps can grow on the white parts of our eyes due to too much sun exposure. These usually appear as we get older and can affect our eyesight or make our eyes feel uncomfortable. This is why we need to wear sunglasses to protect our eyes.

Skin Cancers

2 out of every 3 people in Australia will get a skin cancer during their lifetime. Small skin cancers can often be removed by a doctor. Sadly, some people die from getting these sorts of cancers.

Q. & A.

Q. I have pale skin and I feel silly having to wear a long sleeved top when I go swimming. Everyone else just lies in the sun and gets suntanned.

A. When you are older you will be glad you were sensible now. Hopefully you will avoid getting skin cancers from the sun, unlike those people who are happy to let the sun burn them. Suntanned skin goes browner as a response to burning.

Vitamin D

People need Vitamin D for healthy bones and muscles. Our bodies produce it naturally when the skin is exposed to sunlight. We only need a few minutes each day during the summer to produce enough Vitamin D to keep us healthy.

BUSHFIRES, FLOODS AND CYCLONES

If you are caught in a flooded area, a bushfire or a cyclone, here are some tips on what to do to stay as safe as possible.

Floods

Keep out of flood water. The water can hide snakes or sharp rubbish that can cut your skin and cause infections. Water in a flooded park or street may be rushing down storm water drains beneath the surface. The force of the water could pull you, pets or little children with you down into the drain. Dirty water from overflowing sewerage systems can make floods a source of contamination for anyone who is in the water.

A flooded area is not a place to play, swim or ride a boogie board. If you get into a dangerous situation, emergency service people will have to risk their own lives to come and save you.

People who are not familiar with the bush and the way dry rivers can suddenly fill with water may choose to camp in a dry riverbed. Even if it has not rained in the area, water from a long distance upstream can start flowing and trap anyone who is in its path.

Bushfires

Cyclones

Tropical cyclones occur every year in Australia's northern regions. Listen to the local radio station for cyclone warnings and leave the area early if you can. Camping in the bush if a cyclone is coming is not a good idea.

Cyclones can cause large storm surges, where the sea comes a long way inland. Keep away from the shoreline if there is a cyclone warning.

HOW TO CONTACT EMERGENCY SERVICES IN AUSTRALIA

DO NOT DIAL 911

Have you watched movies and TV shows made in the USA in which people dial 911 for emergencies? This number does not work in Australia, where the emergency number to use is 000.

Emergency+ app

Emergency+ is a free app produced by Australia's emergency services. It uses your phone's GPS system to show on the screen exactly where you are. You can then tell the emergency service your location when you make the 000 call from the app.

1. Dial 000 for police, ambulance and fire brigade.
2. Calmly tell them what is wrong.
3. They will ask where you are. If you do not know the address, tell them as much information as you know.
4. Do not end the call until they tell you to do so.

Dialling 000 from a mobile phone in Australia will still work even if there is no credit left on the phone. You can also make a free 000 call from any pay-phone in Australia.

If you are in a remote location where there is no mobile phone signal, your call will not connect. Anyone going into a remote area should think about getting a mobile satellite phone. This will let them make calls using a satellite connection rather than using signals sent to mobile phone towers. Geolocation emergency devices are available from park rangers in some of Australia's national parks. If a person is bushwalking or camping in a remote area, the geolocator may be the only way to contact emergency services.

FEELING UNSAFE

There's nothing wrong with feeling unsafe and scared. Being scared means that you are sensible enough to know that there is danger around. Being scared is not your fault and you have a right not to feel that way.

Try to think calmly about the safest way to get out of the scary situation you are in.

Shout out for help as long as this will not make the situation worse.

Escape to safety as soon as you can.

Ask a parent or trusted adult to help you.

Call emergency services on the 000 number if necessary.

GLOSSARY

bacteria - tiny, single celled creatures that live all around us
buoyant - able to float
compulsory - required by law or a regulation of some sort
contamination - infection or pollution
dismount - get off a bike or horse
Epipen - medical device used by people with severe allergies
faeces - excrement or 'poo'
feral animal - domestic animal which is living in the wild
rip current - current of water at a beach that takes swimmers away from the shore
SPF rating - Sun Protection Factor rating of a sunscreen product
unpredictable - giving no warning of future actions
unsightly - having a bad appearance

INDEX

Visit these websites to find out more about safety for children:
www.healthykids.nsw.gov.au
www.safety4kids.com.au
www.cancer.org.au
www.cyh.com